Arts at the OLD FIRE STATION Attic

THE LAST NOËL

by

Chris Bush

The Last Noël was first performed at the Merton Arts Space at the Wimbledon Library on 22 November 2019. It transferred to the Old Fire Station, Oxford, on 4 December 2019.

THE LAST NOËL

by

Chris Bush

CAST

TESS	Anna Crichlow
MIKE	Dyfrig Morris
ALICE	Annie Wensak

COMPANY

Director	Jonathan Humphreys
Musical Arrangements and Director	Matt Winkworth
Designer	Alison Neighbour
Lighting Designer	Lucy Adams
Movement Director	Annie-Lunnette Deakin-Foster
Stage Manager	Tessa Gaukroger
Technical Manager	Rachel Luff
Theatre Technician	Cassie White
Producer for Attic	Victoria Hibbs
Producer for AOFS	Alexandra Coke

BIOGRAPHIES

ANNA CRICHLOW | TESS

Anna graduated from the Royal Central School of Speech and Drama in 2016.

She made her professional debut as Kitty Bennet in *Pride & Prejudice* (Regent's Park Open Air), and then completed a run at the National Theatre in *Common*. Further credits include *Confidence* at the Southwark Playhouse and *The Worst Witch* for Royal & Derngate.

She plays the lead in the upcoming short film *Strange Days* directed by Alice Seabright.

DYFRIG MORRIS | MIKE

Theatre includes: *The Jungle Book* (Royal & Derngate/Fiery Angel/CTP); *Henry V* (Regent's Park Open Air Theatre); *Candylion*, *The Misanthrope* (National Theatre Wales); *Richard III*, *James and the Giant Peach* and *Of Mice and Men* (West Yorkshire Playhouse); *The Grand Gesture* (Northern Broadsides); *Rape of the Fair Country*, *As You Like It*, *A Small Family Business*, *Arden of Faversham*, *Festen*, *A Midsummer Night's Dream*, *Jack and the Beanstalk*, *Beauty and the Beast*, *The Grapes of Wrath*, *Troilus and Cressida*, *Hobson's Choice*, *Waiting for Godot*, *One Flew Over the Cuckoo's Nest*, *Aladdin*, *The Crucible*, *Silas Marner* and *Rosencrantz & Guildenstern Are Dead*

(Clwyd Theatr Cymru); *Wizard of Oz* (Hull Truck Theatre); *Cinderella*, *Sleeping Beauty* and *Aladdin* (Leeds City Varieties); *The Constant Wife* (Salisbury Playhouse); *Edward II* and *Dr Faustus* (Royal Exchange Theatre, Manchester); *The Nutcracker* (Theatre Royal Bath Productions); *Crackers Christmas* (Sherman Theatre Company); *The Twits* (Belgrade Coventry); *Y Madogwys* (Dalier Sylw); *Bully for You* (Roundabout); *Jekyll & Mr. Hyde* (Equinox).

Television includes: *The Crown* (Netflix), *Hinterland/Y Gwyll*, *Gwaith Cartref* and *Y Pris* (Fiction Factory), *Spilt Milk/Cara Fi* (Touchpaper Television), *Desperate Romantics* (BBC 2), *Dau Dy A Ni* (Boomerang/HTV), *Tightrope Pictures* (BBC), *Treflan* (Alfresco), *Pobl-y-Cwm* (BBC Wales), *Glan Hafren* (HTV).

Film includes: *The Big I Am* (TBIAFLIX), *Lois* (Ffilmiau Eryri).

Radio includes: *Like the First Dewfall* and *The Great Chocolate Murders* (BBC Radio Drama).

ANNIE WENSAK | ALICE

Annie trained at Arts Educational Schools.

Theatre includes: *The Children* (English Speaking Theatre Frankfurt); *Moll Flanders* (Mercury Theatre, Colchester); *The Rhythm Method* (Bush Theatre); *Half A Sixpence* (Noël Coward Theatre/Chichester Festival Theatre); *Beyond The Fence* (Arts Theatre); *The Stationmaster* (Tristan Bates Theatre); *Seven Brides for Seven Brothers* (Regent's Park Open Air Theatre); *The Sound of Music* (Leicester Curve); *Sister Act* (Kilworth House); *White Christmas* (Cardiff Millennium Centre/Edinburgh Playhouse); *Singin' in the Rain* (Courtyard Theatre, Hereford); *My Fair Lady*

(Plenary Hall Kuala Lumpur); *Jailhouse Rock* (Piccadilly Theatre); *Supposed to Live* (Pleasance Theatre); *The Tree Dream* (Norwich Playhouse); *Two Men from Derby*, *Happy End*, *Cabaret* (Library Theatre Manchester); *Marry Me A Little* (Edinburgh Festival).

Annie has toured nationally in *Oliver!*, *Double Death*, *Spend, Spend, Spend* and *Tess of the d'Urbervilles*. European tours include: *An Inspector Calls* and *Twelfth Night*.

Television includes: *Beyond The Fence* (Sky TV); *The Bill* (ITV); *Casualty*, *Crimewatch UK*, *Pennies from Heaven* (BBC).

CHRIS BUSH | WRITER

Chris Bush is a Sheffield-born playwright, lyricist and theatremaker. Past work includes *Pericles* (Olivier, National Theatre); *A Declaration from the People* (Dorfman, National Theatre); *The Changing Room* (National Theatre Connections Festival); *The Assassination of Katie Hopkins* (Theatr Clwyd); *Standing at the Sky's Edge, Steel, What We Wished For, A Dream, The Sheffield Mysteries, 20 Tiny Plays about Sheffield* (Sheffield Theatres); *Scenes from the End of the World* (CSSD: Yard Theatre); *Transcending* (Orange Tree Theatre); *Larksong* (New Vic Theatre); *Cards on the Table* (Royal Exchange Theatre); *ODD* (Royal & Derngate, Northampton: concert performance); *Sleight & Hand* (Summerhall/ Odeon Cinemas/BBC Arts); *TONY! The Blair Musical* (York Theatre Royal/tour); *Speaking Freely, Poking the Bear* (Theatre503); *The Bureau of Lost Things* (Theatre503/Rose Bruford) and *Wolf* (Latitude Festival). Chris has won the National Young Playwrights' Festival, a Brit Writers' Award and the Perfect Pitch Award. She has previously been Playwright in Residence for Sheffield Theatres, and part of writers' groups at the National Theatre, Orange Tree and Royal Exchange, Manchester.

JONATHAN HUMPHREYS | DIRECTOR

Jonathan is Artistic Director of Attic and a freelance director. He trained at Drama Centre London before working as an assistant director at the National Theatre and RSC. He was awarded the Regional Young Theatre Director bursary to Sheffield Theatres where his work has received widespread critical acclaim and his production of Beckett's *Happy Days* won a TMA Award.

His recent productions includes: *The Death of Ivan Ilyich, The Rebellious Women of Wimbledon* (Attic); *The Rivals* (The Watermill); *The Orestia* (RADA); *The Mighty Walzer* (Royal Exchange Theatre, Manchester); *Romeo and Juliet, Boeing Boeing, The Village Bike* (Sheffield Theatres); *Oscar Wilde on Trial* (Reading Between the Lines/Reading Gaol); *The Hotel Plays* (Defibrillator/Langham Hotel). His first short film, *The Send Off*, was commissioned by BBC and has played at festivals internationally.

For the last two years he was Associate Director for National Theatre Connections, an annual youth theatre programme working with over 5000 young people across the UK.

MATT WINKWORTH | MUSICAL ARRANGEMENTS AND DIRECTOR

Matt is an Oxford-born composer. He was artist-in-residence at The Oxford Playhouse 2016–17, won the KSF Artist of Choice award in 2015 and the Perfect Pitch Award in 2014.

Recent credits include: *The Assassination of Katie Hopkins* (Theatr Clwyd; UK Theatre Award Best New Musical); *Elves and the Shoemaker* (Jacquline du Pré, Oxford); *High As Sugar* (Brighton Fringe/King's Head Theatre, OFS); *Death and Chocolate* (Lost Theatre); *Nell Gwynn, Attempts On Her Life, Under Milk Wood, Animal Farm* (Oxford Playhouse Young Company); *The Bureau of Lost Things* (Theatre503); *ODD* (Perfect Pitch/Royal & Derngate, Northampton: concert performance).

ALISON NEIGHBOUR | DESIGNER

Alison is a scenographer working in theatre, dance, installation and site responsive practice. Her work includes text-based, devised, and self-led projects, often working closely with communities and found spaces or outdoor environments. Alison trained at RADA and is represented by The Designer's Formation. She is also a resident at Pervasive Media Studio and founder of Bread & Goose.

Recent work includes: *Gulp!* (national tour); *Collapsible* (Assembly Roxy; Hightide; Dublin Fringe; Bush Theatre); *Egin* (National Theatre Wales residency); *The Girl With Incredibly Long Hair* (Welsh tour); *Good Girl* (Trafalgar Studios); *Tumulus* (Soho Theatre); *The Hotel Experience* (UK tour); *The Little Prince* (Playground Theatre); *Return* (Dunraven Bay outdoor community project); *Hanging in the Balance, Spectra* (mac, Birmingham); *Constellations, A Peter Rabbit Tale* (Singapore Repertory Theatre); *Ross & Rachel* (UK tour); *Spine* (UK tour); *The Curtain* (Young Vic); *Phenomenal People* (Fuel, UK tour); *Lost in the Neuron Forest* (UK tour); *The Memory Store* (UK tour); *The Eyes Have It* (Imagine Watford Festival); *Crazy Gary's Mobile Disco* (Chapter Arts Centre & Wales tour).

LUCY ADAMS | LIGHTING DESIGNER

Lucy Adams is a London based lighting designer working in devised work and new writing. She's an associate artist with ThisEgg, having designed *Goggles, Me and My Bee, UNCONDITIONAL* and *dressed.* (Fringe First Award winner) for the company. Other theatre includes: *It's True, It's True, It's True,* (BREACH Theatre; Fringe First Award winner); *Art Heist* (Poltergeist Theatre/Edinburgh Fringe/New Diorama Theatre); *Anyone's Guess How We Got Here* (Barrel Organ/Edinburgh Fringe); *The Accident Did Not Take Place* and *[insert slogan here]* (YESYESNONO/Edinburgh Fringe); *Bottom* (Willy Hudson/Edinburgh Fringe/Soho Theatre); *Ex-Boyfriend Yard Sale* (Haley McGee/Camden People's Theatre) and *Cult of K*nzo* (Paula Varjack/UK tour).

Her lighting design for new writing includes *Skin A Cat* by Isley Lynn directed by Blythe Stewart (UK tour); *One Jewish Boy* by Stephen Laughton directed by Sarah Meadows (Old Red Lion); *A Hundred Words for Snow* by Tatty Hennessy directed by Lucy Atkinson (VAULT Festival and Trafalgar Studios) and *The Amber Trap* by Tabitha Mortiboy directed by Hannah Hauer-King (Theatre503).

ANNIE-LUNNETTE DEAKIN-FOSTER | MOVEMENT DIRECTOR | CHOREOGRAPHER

Annie-Lunnette Deakin-Foster is a passionate contemporary dance theatre choreographer, maker and movement director, and was a founding member of award-winning company, C-12 Dance Theatre.

Recent theatre credits include: *Pavilion* by Emily White dir. by Tamara Harvey (Theatr Clwyd); *Chiaroscuro* by Jackie Kay dir. by Lynette Linton (Bush Theatre); *On The Other Hand We're Happy* by Daf James, *Daughterhood* by Charley Miles and *Dexter & Winter's Detective Agency* by Nathan Byron dir. by Stef Driscoll (ROUNDABOUT); *Aesop's Fables* by Justin Audibert and Rachel Bagshaw (Unicorn Theatre); *You Stupid Darkness* by Sam Steiner dir. by James Grieve (Theatre Royal Plymouth); *Grimm Tales* – Philip Pullman's collection adapted by Philip Wilson dir. by Kirsty Housley (Unicorn Theatre); *Jericho's Rose* by Althea Theatre (The Hope & Anchor); *Pop Music* by Anna Jordan dir. by James Grieve (Barry Jackson/national tour); *The Court Must Have a Queen* by Ade Solanke directed by Sam Curtis Lindsay (Hampton Court Palace); *These Bridges* by Phoebe Éclair-Powell (WCYT as part of National Theatre Connections at the Bush Theatre); *The Little Match Girl and Other Happier Tales* by Joel Horwood and Emma Rice (2016–2017 Shakespeare's Globe and presented by Bristol Old Vic 2017–2018 then toured nationally). *The Dark Room* by Angela Betzien (Theatre503). For more information check out: www.annielunnettedeakinfoster.com.

Recent dance credits include: *Force* (Abbey Road Studios/Imagine Festival Watford, Greenwich & Docklands International Festival/Netherlands); *Shhh!* (Dance City, MAC Birmingham/Norwich Playhouse/The Woodville Gravesend/CircoMedia Bristol, Winchester Theatre Royal).

TESSA GAUKROGER | PRODUCTION STAGE MANAGER

Tessa trained at Cygnet Training Theatre, Exeter.

Previous production management roles include *Where the Lines are Drawn, Kiss'n'Tell* (Little Fish Theatre, South London tour); *Murder, She Didn't Write* (Degrees of Error, The Pleasance at Edinburgh Fringe/UK tour) as well as five separate UK tours (*The Way I Look, The Good Stuff, O&O Don't Do Edinburgh)* for her own award-winning company, O&O.

The Old Fire Station has been a popular Oxford venue for many years but since it was refurbished and re-opened in 2011, it has become something extra special.

In just eight years, we have created a popular thriving multi-form arts centre presenting work by the best small-scale touring companies as well as local talent, organising festivals such as Offbeat (our own mini Edinburgh Fringe) and mounting a varied programme of exhibitions in the gallery and elsewhere. We host around 20 regular dance classes every week and have a gorgeous shop selling contemporary craft and feel-good gifts. We also support artists by offering studio space and help with creative and technical processes and in marketing, fundraising, selling and networking. We now have a distinctive artistic offer to the public as a receiving house, a curator and a producer and, through close partnership working, we have become a hub for artists of all disciplines to test ideas, make and showcase great work.

But what makes us extra special is that we share our building with the homelessness charity Crisis. Through this partnership, we've developed a nationally recognised model of social inclusion – enabling people facing tough times to see shows, volunteer, train, get paid work, create art and help run the arts centre.

And we think deeply about what we are doing and what impact we are having – mainly by asking people to tell us stories about what change has happened for them and how.

Our spaces are intimate, inspiring, professional and accessible to all. The public comes to drink coffee, buy art, attend classes and watch shows. Homeless people come to learn, gain skills and get support. Artists come to rehearse, create and showcase. They all come through the same door and find themselves sharing space and interests. We focus on good quality relationships, encouraging creativity and risk-taking, and offering a truly inclusive public space.

Oxford is globally renowned for stunning heritage and outstanding research. But it's also a place of disadvantage and inequality.

Oxford needs the Old Fire Station because it is about openness, inclusion, looking forward and different thinking. The Old Fire Station acts as a bridge between sectors, organisations and people.

We need friends to support us so, if you'd like to know more about what happens at the Old Fire Station, just get in touch or find out more here: www.oldfirestation.org.uk

WHAT WE DO

Presenting new work across art forms – we want our reputation to be good quality art aimed at adults which takes a risk, asks questions and entertains. We want our audiences to have fun and be open to new ideas and different people.

Supporting artists – we support early to mid-career artists from all disciplines with advice, networks and promotion to help them become more successful.

Including people facing tough times – we share our building with the homelessness charity, Crisis. Through this partnership, we offer people who are homeless space to define themselves and choose their own labels by including them in the running of the centre - as audience, participants, volunteers and co-creators. We look for ways of including those who are socially isolated and disadvantaged. This improves the quality of what we do, helps develop networks, builds resilience and leads to more stable lives.

We do this, with Crisis, by offering a public space which is shared by very different people and helps to break down barriers and promote solidarity in Oxford.

Back in 2016, Jonny Donahoe created our first ever Christmas show for grown-ups, *30 Christmases*, with Paddy Gervers and Rachel Parris. The following year Jonny wrote *Working Christmas* for us with James Rowland and, in 2018, he introduced us to his old friend, Mike Bartlett, who created the brilliant and hugely successful *Snowflake* to great critical acclaim. So, in 2019, we were faced with the daunting challenge of finding a Christmas show that could build on the fantastic work of both Jonny and Mike. And along came Chris Bush.

Thank you, Jonny Humphreys and Attic Theatre Company, for co-producing and directing the piece so beautifully and to the amazing cast and crew. Thanks also to Arts Council England, Backstage Trust, New Diorama and Windich Legal for supporting the show.

The Last Noël is fantastic storytelling and beautiful songs helping us access what matters most about being human. There will be tears as we remember people we miss at Christmas and the people we love and there will be laughter as we recognise ourselves in the characters. Most of all it will help us celebrate that tricky, joyful, poignant, silly, complicated and deeply meaningful thing that is Christmas.

oldfirestation.org.uk

Attic

Attic is an arts organisation based in South London.

We like to think of ourselves as a local theatre or arts centre without walls: we make theatre of the highest quality whilst always maintaining a strong and active relationship with to our local community, in Mitcham, south London and its surrounding areas.

We do this through two complimentary approaches:

Making for work for: commissioning and producing new, relevant and inclusive theatre which speaks to both local and national audiences

Making work with: developing and delivering participation projects which nurture the creativity of ordinary people.

We work hard to make everyone feel welcome at whatever we do, and invigorated and enriched by their experience of our work.

Our original shows are created in collaboration with leading artists and place the reaching of new, cross generational audiences at their heart. As such, we often show work in libraries, community spaces or site specific settings, as well as theatres, to make sure our work is as accessible as possible.

In the last five years our work has included *Fields Unsown* by Catherine Harvey and Louise Monaghan, a specially commissioned promenade piece to mark the centenary of WWI at Morden Hall Park; the world premiere of *Beacons* by Tabitha Mortiboy at the Park Theatre; a tour of *The Rebellious Women of Wimbledon* by Beth Flintoff, a new play which explored our local history of the suffragette movement and an adaptation of Leo Tolstoy's *The Death of Ivan Ilyich* by Stephen Sharkey. Following *The Last Noël* our next project will be the world premiere of a new commission, *All Roads* by Roy Williams OBE.

As important to us as our shows, is our inclusive and vibrant arts participation programme with people of all ages in our local area of Mitcham; we work with hundreds of people each year. Recent and regular projects include free creative arts and film making workshops for young people, workshops that promote confidence for those newly arrived in the UK or struggling to cope, elders singing and dance groups, and a Christmas project with members of a local sheltered living scheme.

The idea for this show began with a desire to create a new play with music to tour to our local area, aimed particularly at those who, for whatever reason, might not have the chance to experience theatre regularly. I have loved Chris Bush's work for a long time (it is heartfelt, funny and uplifting, and has the remarkable ability to communicate the most complex, deep and human experiences, in the most entertaining and unexpected way) so we approached her for a commission. She has a pretty impressive track record of making work with music, having won Best Musical at the UK Theatre Awards the last two years running (the first of which she shared with our incredible musical director Matt Winkworth), and her plays have been performed at many of leading theatres most notably the National. As we discussed what the show could be, it became clear she had a wonderful idea for a grown up Christmas show; thus, *The Last Noël* began to evolve.

Working with such a brilliant writer is very exciting for us, as it enables us to take a world premiere to libraries and community venues all over South London, and increase access to great new theatre for all. However, being so proud of the piece, we were really keen to share it with an even wider audience. We were therefore delighted when we began talking with Arts at the Old Fire Station about the show coming to them, following the wonderful Snowflake and building upon their track record of 'grown up' festive shows. As co-producers, AOFS felt like a great match, sharing our commitment to inclusion for all, which is highlighted through their inspiring partnership with Crisis, and aligns so closely with the aims of our community participation work. We couldn't be happier with AOFS as a perfect second home for our show.

The future of all our work is, as for so many charities and arts organisation, highly uncertain. Whilst we are very grateful for the continued, regular support of Merton Council and Marcus Beale Architects in Wimbledon, all our work relies on income raised from trusts, foundations and individuals which is becoming increasingly challenging. To find out more about our work, and how you might help, get in touch or check out our website.

We are immensely grateful to Arts Council England, Cockayne: Grants for the Arts, London Community Foundation, the Leche Trust and the Royal Victoria Hall Foundation for their support with this show. Without it, it simply wouldn't have happened.

And, of course, a very Merry Christmas.

www.attictheatrecompany.com

Artistic Director: Jonathan Humphreys
General Manager: Victoria Hibbs
Creative Engagement Producer: Bryony Farrant-Davis

THE LAST NOËL

Chris Bush

For Mum

Foreword

I've wanted to write a Christmas show for years, for the simple
reason that Christmas is magic: however old and cynical I get
I don't think that will ever change. It's also, for me, a holiday
detached from any religious significance, but one steeped in ritual
all the same. Now is not the time for revolution or reinvention
(let's keep those promises for New Year), but instead it's when
we build upon and refine the traditions we've spent a lifetime
developing. We all have our own seasonal idiosyncrasies, and
while they might seem absurd to outsiders, to forsake them would
be unthinkable. So, this year I will bake biscotti for my family,
I will drink expensive cocktails with my friend Lucy that neither
of us can afford, I will read from a book of Jeanette Winterson
short stories each night before bed (I know, I'm insufferable, but
let me have this). I shall overeat and watch *Robbie the Reindeer*
and fight a losing battle for a tastefully decorated tree.

My perfect Yuletide might not look anything like yours, but
'perfect' has no place here anyway. Christmas is messy in the
way that love is messy, and people are messy (and festive craft
projects that looked totally feasible on Pinterest are messy). If
The Last Noël is a show about the true meaning of Christmas, at
first glance this might appear to boil down to alcohol, arguments
and preposterously flavoured seasonal crisps, but of course
there's more to it than that. It's about hope and song and keeping
a lantern burning. It's about a family trying to tell the story of
who they are through the traditions they've built together. It's
about the pull of the familiar and the inevitability of change.

Christmas is for family, but family can mean anything. If we're
lucky, it's the time of year where we get to gather together the
people we love and celebrate with them. One of the beautiful
things about touring this show around community spaces and
then settling in at The Old Fire Station is we can try and break
down some of the more formal barriers associated with a night
out at the theatre. As these rooms open their doors to us, we in
turn offer you a seat at our table. We'll dim the lights and tell

you a story (or three), and hopefully emerge a little closer by the time we're done. We can all be family for the hour or so we spend together, and that might just be the best gift I can offer.

Merry Christmas.

Chris Bush,
November 2019

Characters

ALICE, *sixties, retired, mother of:*
MIKE, *forty-one, graphic designer, uncle of:*
TESS, *nineteen, university student*

Plus, in all likelihood, an additional PIANIST/MD. If actors can also play some instruments, all the better.

This text went to press before the end of rehearsals and so may differ slightly from the play as performed.

A kitchen/living space decked out in Christmas finery. The decorations on display have been accumulated over decades. This is a warm and practical space which gets plenty of use.

A feast is being prepared. ALICE *is nominally in charge/ supervising, while* MIKE *is taking a more hands-on approach.* TESS *is mostly trying to eat things without getting told off and making sure everything is just the way she likes it.*

As the audience are seated, they might be offered drinks/snacks, and recruited to help with peeling potatoes, prepping canapés, etc. Perhaps they're encouraged to join in with a festive sing-song, and/or their opinions might be sought on various contentious Christmas matters – sprouts or no sprouts? Presents before or after dinner? The Snowman *or the Queen's Speech? Each family member is delighted when they find someone who agrees with them, and there's a friendly rivalry between them. The most important thing is that the audience are our guests, and they're made to feel welcome.*

Once everyone is settled, music shifts into the opening number.

Song: 'It's Christmas'

MIKE. IT ISN'T ABOUT
    WHETHER YOU LIKE SPROUTS
    SPROUTS AREN'T THERE FOR YOU TO LIKE THEM
    IT'S TRADITION
    AND WE COULDN'T DO WITHOUT

    IT ISN'T THE TIME
    TO PLAY FAST AND LOOSE
    WITH YOUR FLAVOUR COMBINATIONS
    THE TIME FOR EXPERIMENTATION
    IS NOT TODAY

    THERE'S AN ANGEL ON THE TREE
    I MADE IN 1983
    WHEN I WALK IN IF I CAN'T SEE IT
    I'LL KICK OFF

    IT'S CHRISTMAS

ALICE *picks up the song.*

ALICE. IT ISN'T ABOUT
    WHEN THEY CALLED YOU LAST
    THEY DON'T NEED TO GIVE A REASON
    'TIS THE SEASON
    WHEN WE LEAVE THINGS IN THE PAST

    IT ISN'T ABOUT
    GETTING EVERYTHING RIGHT
    LIFE'S TOO SHORT TO TRY
    TO KEEP UP WITH NIGELLA
    OR WHOEVER THE HELL
    THEY MIGHT BE WATCHING

    MINE'S A SHERRY, MINE'S A GIN
    TAKE OFF YOUR SHOES WHEN YOU COME IN
    IS YOUR NAME JESUS –
    WERE YOU BROUGHT UP IN A BARN?

ALICE/MIKE. MERRY CHRISTMAS

TESS, *dragging a large gym bag full of washing, takes over.*

TESS. IT ISN'T ABOUT
    SNEAKING OUT
    TO THE PUB TO SEE YOUR MATES
    TO HAVE THE SAME OLD CONVERSATIONS
    YOU HAD LAST YEAR ANYWAY

    IT ISN'T ABOUT
    THE ROWING MACHINE
    THAT'S APPEARED IN YOUR ROOM
    IT FEELS TOO SOON
    IT'S ALL TOO SOON

    BUT RING THE BELLS AND SING OF CHEER
    YES I STILL NEED A STOCKING THIS YEAR
    SOME THINGS SHOULD NEVER CHANGE

    LIKE CHRISTMAS

The three overlap.

    RING OUT THOSE BELLS
MIKE.   WHO'S MOVED THE CHESTNUTS?

ALICE.   CAN YOU PUT THAT DOWN PLEASE?
TESS. SING OF CHRISTMAS TIME
MIKE.   MUM? MUM! MUM?!
ALICE.   THEY'RE FOR LATER
TESS. AND ALL THE TREATS WE ONLY GET
     AND DO WE HAVE THE BISCUITS THAT I LIKE?
MIKE.   I JUST HAD THEM
ALICE.   AM I TALKING TO MYSELF?

ALL. RING OUT THOSE BELLS
     SING OF CHRISTMAS TIME
     AND ALL THE STUPID LITTLE THINGS
     THAT MEAN THE WORLD TO US

     THAT'S CHRISTMAS.

Song ends. They address the audience.

ALICE. Today –

TESS. [*States today's date.*]

MIKE. Today is Christmas Day.

TESS. Admittedly not the traditional date associated with Christmas Day, but –

ALICE. But this year, this is when it falls.

MIKE. In our family we have a roving Christmas – a bit like Easter, how Easter fluctuates depending on... on...

TESS. Go on.

MIKE. Y'know, equinoxes? Or...

TESS. Uh-huh.

MIKE. Lunar, um... Whitsun, solstice... I don't know. Mum?

ALICE *shrugs.*

Right. Anyway, not the point. Oh, but should we – ?

ALICE. What?

MIKE. Introductions?

ALICE. Yes. Right. Hello – I'm Alice – this is my son Michael –

MIKE. Mike –

ALICE. My granddaughter Tessa.

TESS. And he's – (*Re:* MIKE.) my uncle, not my dad, just to –

MIKE. Yep. And the person missing – the person we're waiting for – is Gail, who is my big sister, and – (*Re:* TESS.) her mum, and – (*Re:* ALICE.) her daughter. And –

TESS. And waiting for my dad too.

MIKE. Yeah. I mean I think we all care a little bit less about him, but –

TESS. Nice.

MIKE. But – but actually the pair of them are the reason for all this. The roving Christmas is all her fault, basically.

ALICE. Don't.

MIKE. It is.

ALICE. It is not.

TESS. No, it sort of is. You see when your mum is a doctor and your dad is a paramedic you learn to be a bit more flexible with your holiday dates.

ALICE. We never know when we're going to be able to get everyone in the same room together, so –

MIKE. And of course the rest of us are expected to just drop everything and make ourselves available.

TESS. You work from home.

MIKE. That's not the point.

TESS. Pretty sure it is.

ALICE. Let's not bicker.

MIKE. My time is just as important as –

TESS. Is it though?

ALICE. Anyway. The point is we find a date where everyone's available –

MIKE. We're told.

ALICE. And that becomes our Christmas. And in a way, it makes it more special.

TESS. Really doesn't when you're eight, but –

ALICE. Because Christmas is, ultimately, Christmas is about –

MIKE. Christmas was inside us all along!

ALICE. Can you take this seriously?

MIKE. Who'd like a drink? Who'd like a nibble?

TESS. Who'd like a preposterously flavoured seasonal crisp?

ALICE. They're not for yet!

MIKE. Mum!

ALICE. We can open them when your sister gets here.

MIKE. No – that is not the rule for canapés!

ALICE. They won't be long.

MIKE. Canapés are a pre-dinner snack.

ALICE. You can have a piece of fruit if you must have something.

MIKE. Unbelievable.

TESS. Hold on, I've got train snacks. I've got... (*Going through pockets*.) Yep. I've got a quarter pack of Tangfastics and some seed mix.

ALICE. Put those away.

TESS. Not going to lie, I have been sitting on them.

MIKE. The house is literally full of food.

ALICE. You don't want to spoil your appetite anyway.

MIKE. They're *appetisers*, the whole point is to... (*Gives up*.) Every year.

ALICE (*to* TESS). Have you heard from your father?

TESS. He messaged me when he was setting off. (*Checks phone*.) Nothing else. That's normal. Hard to know how long he'll be waiting.

ALICE. But that was all – ?

TESS. Fine. Yeah, I think fine.

MIKE. So. So they are on their way, or they will be soon, and when they finally deign to arrive – because she's the favourite, obviously –

ALICE. That isn't –

MIKE. And the world revolves around her –

ALICE. Stop it.

MIKE. Then the festivities can properly commence. And the important thing, the most crucial rule – and apologies for this in advance – is that we have the smallest possible amount of fun before she gets here, so she doesn't feel like she's missed out on anything.

ALICE. That isn't true.

TESS. Actually that is very true.

ALICE. She just likes to be included.

MIKE. One year I opened a box of Christmas Tree shortbread in the morning and she didn't speak to me until after trifle.

TESS. Are we having trifle this year?

MIKE. Of course we are.

TESS. Yes!

ALICE. But as we're waiting –

MIKE. As we're waiting we tell stories.

TESS. Old stories. Familiar stories.

ALICE. Stories that can be told and retold.

MIKE. And no one can get upset if they miss out, because they've heard them a hundred times before.

TESS. And that's what we do. Our pre-arrival tradition.

MIKE. The smallest amount of fun that's allowed.

ALICE. And we tell her favourite story.

TESS. And it's okay that she isn't here for it, because it will get told again.

MIKE. And her favourite story is:

They all speak at once.

ALICE. / 'The Lighthouse Keeper'.

MIKE. / 'The Three Best Men'.

TESS. / 'The Night Before Christmas'.

MIKE. Every year!

TESS. They're both wrong.

ALICE. I know my own daughter's favourite story.

MIKE. No, you think you do, but she's just too polite to tell you otherwise.

TESS. Well it's definitely not yours.

MIKE. It is – of course it is – it's about her!

TESS. Actually it's about you.

MIKE. Maybe a bit, but –

ALICE. Absurd story – utter nonsense.

MIKE. And – now hold on – (*To* TESS.) 'The Night Before Christmas' is about you, isn't it – the way she tells it? It's not the proper story at all.

TESS. Exactly – the way *she* tells it, because *I'm* her favourite. And   ergo – it is therefore her favourite story. Boom. (*Launching in.*) 'Twas the –

ALICE. No, sweetheart, it honestly isn't.

MIKE. And don't say 'boom'.

TESS. It is! The whole point is that it's a Mum original – or a, uh, what's the word? A reimagining. She made it up – it's *her* story. (*To audience.*) It's great – you'll see. (*Tries again.*) 'Twas the night before –

MIKE. No, no, no – hold on – leave them out of it –

TESS. Why?

MIKE. I will not have this anarchy.

ALICE. Can we try not to squabble, please?

TESS. He started it.

ALICE. There's no need for an argument.

MIKE. That's what Christmas is for.

ALICE. No, Christmas is for family.

TESS. Same difference.

MIKE *smirks*.

ALICE. If we're all just going to descend into silliness –

MIKE. Mum –

ALICE. If it's going to cause an upset, if you're both going to get agitated, maybe it's better not to tell any of them at all.

MIKE. Come on.

ALICE. I'm serious.

TESS. So what, are we all just going to sit here in silence?

ALICE. No – there's plenty of other things we could discuss. I want to hear about university, about how you're getting on, because Belinda – you know Belinda from over the...? She was showing me how I could find your... your twitters, and I did have some questions about –

TESS. Granny, I will literally pay you to tell the story of 'The Lighthouse Keeper' right now. Please.

ALICE. Without interruption?

TESS. I promise.

ALICE. Michael?

MIKE. I'm opening a packet of crisps and there's nothing you can do to stop me.

ALICE. Please yourself. But don't crunch.

MIKE (*to* TESS). Want one?

TESS. What are they?

MIKE (*reading the packet*). Christingle Orange.

TESS. You're alright.

ALICE. Right – if we're all sitting comfortably? Then I'll begin.

ALICE *slips easily into a cosily dramatic 'storytelling' mode. Underscore begins.*

This is the story as I would tell it to my daughter, as my mother would tell it to me, and her mother to her before that. As such, the story changes with the times, with the tides, which is fitting, because it takes place at sea.

TESS. So good. It is properly good actually.

ALICE. The story is remembered by the ocean – borne aloft on the crest of waves and whispered into seashells on far-flung beaches. And like the ever-changing river, it is never the same story twice.

TESS. Bit Pocahontas, but go on.

ALICE *sighs.*

(*To* MIKE.) Crisp me.

MIKE. You sure?

TESS *eats a crisp and immediately regrets it.*

TESS. Eurgh.

ALICE. Ahem. And this is how the story always starts: There is a lighthouse. A lighthouse sitting in the middle of the wine-dark sea.

MIKE. Ink-black sea.

ALICE. Hmm?

MIKE. Ink-black.

TESS. What does 'wine-dark' actually mean?

ALICE. Wine-dark is… It's Homeric. Poetic.

MIKE. It's idiotic.

ALICE. I thought we had an understanding –

MIKE. And just to… Not to… But lighthouses aren't actually in the middle of the sea, are they – wine-dark or otherwise? They're on the coast.

ALICE. Fine. I'll stop.

TESS. No –

ALICE (*to* MIKE). Your sister never interrupts.

MIKE. I'm not – I won't – I promise.

TESS. Please. We'll be good. Please.

ALICE (*sighs*). Fine. (*To* MIKE.) Pour me a brandy.

TESS. Now we're talking. (*To* MIKE.) Baileys please.

   MIKE *rolls his eyes but goes to pour drinks*.

ALICE. So. There is a lighthouse.
   Sitting in a wine-dark sea
   The water, cold as a choc-ice.

TESS. Yes!

ALICE. Black like molasses –

MIKE. She used to say 'black as sin', but we decided that was
   almost definitely racist.

   ALICE *ignores this*.

ALICE. Water that licks at the stone steps
   Crashes against the curved walls
   Hammers on the door with the fury of a spurned lover.

MIKE. Nice – is that new?

ALICE. There is a lighthouse sitting in a wine-dark sea
   And the cold surrounds it like sharks circling
   But inside, a light is blazing
   And there is a small, round living room
   Welcoming and warm
   And it smells of Christmas,
   Of clove and orange and ruby-red wine –

MIKE. Normal-coloured wine then?

ALICE. A pudding wrapped in muslin
   Is simmering on the stove
   And there in a well-worn armchair
   Sits the lighthouse keeper
   And she is waiting
   Because sometimes there is nothing to do but wait

And keep a light burning
Sometimes that is the only thing to do.

She stops.

TESS. Pause for dramatic effect. Love it.

ALICE (*distracted*). Sorry. Sorry, it's not –

MIKE. It's okay.

ALICE. Maybe enough for right now.

MIKE. Are you – ?

ALICE. Actually – actually why don't we open some…? Maybe
    I am a little peckish. And you do never know, do you, how
    long… So I think –

MIKE. Absolutely.

    ALICE *moves away and starts rummaging for snacks.* TESS
    fills the silence.

TESS (*out*). So – little bit of festive feminist analysis for you on
    how the story's going so far – female lighthouse keeper –
    tick – full marks for that. But she is waiting, which is quite
    a passive activity, and she is waiting for a man –

MIKE. Spoiler alert –

TESS. Yeah. Which also isn't ideal. That isn't really a spoiler,
    that's the next bit. She's waiting for her husband – her lover –
    and there was a period in my childhood when Mum swapped
    the husband to a wife to sort of casually start teaching me
    about same-sex relationships, which was… was a bit weird.

MIKE. Homophobe.

TESS. Not because… just because I knew the story already, so
    I wanted to know what'd happened to her husband, why did
    she have a wife now, all of a sudden? What had…? Not
    against it in principle, but –

MIKE. Wasn't my idea, by the way.

TESS. Hmm?

MIKE. In case you –

TESS. Right – yes, right! Exactly. I had a gay uncle already –
I had a handle on that. Lesbian lighthouse keepers felt
superfluous. Anyway.

ALICE (*calling over*). I'm going to make tea – does anyone
want tea?

MIKE. I thought you were on the booze now.

ALICE. I just fancy a… a –

TESS. I could do it.

ALICE. No, it's alright.

ALICE *starts making tea.*

MIKE. Right. So we're just taking a… a little hiatus from
lighthouse keepers, just for a moment, so… No, good. Great.
So – 'The Three Best Men'. December 27th, 1998 –

TESS. Oh, you're just jumping in, are you?

MIKE. I'm jumping in.

TESS. Okay.

MIKE. I'm seizing the moment.

TESS. Great.

MIKE. I'm embracing the anarchy.

TESS. Knock yourself out.

MIKE. So, okay. So it's December 27th, 1998. I am twenty
years old. The Spice Girls are enjoying their third
consecutive Christmas Number One. And in just a few hours'
time my big sister is getting married.

ALICE (*calling over*). Anybody else?

TESS. No thanks.

MIKE. Now, for those paying attention you might've noticed
the date – December 27th, yes. And to confirm your next
thought, also yes, people who get married at Christmas are
universally dickheads.

ALICE. There's really no need for –

MIKE. But as we've already established, my sister has never had a problem with making everything about her.

TESS. It was her wedding!

MIKE. It was my Christmas! And people who get married at Christmas, they say 'oh, well the family will be getting together anyway – it's *convenient*' – no – it's convenient for *you* – for everyone else you have actually, actually just hijacked the holidays, so –

TESS. And you still think this is Mum's favourite story, do you?

MIKE. I'm getting there.

ALICE. I thought it was wonderful. And that gap between Christmas and New Year – no one knows what to do with themselves anyway.

MIKE. I have been – with no disrespect to anyone – dying to get back to Manchester, where I'm at university, and where I am deeply in love with a boy called Dean Whitehead, who quotes Philip Larkin and dresses like Liam Gallagher, and for some reason that is what does it for me at the time.

TESS. Tragic.

MIKE. Quiet.

ALICE. Oh, I think I met him.

MIKE. You did meet him. It was a car wreck.

ALICE. I don't think I saw the appeal.

MIKE. You weren't meant to.

TESS. Another side note – bit of trivia for you – generally speaking the three of us have very different tastes in men –

MIKE. As you'd hope.

TESS. Right, yes – but to date we've only found one man who we all unequivocally agree on. Any guesses? Anyone? No? Mark Ruffalo. So.

MIKE. Can't argue with it.

ALICE. Not when he's green, but...

MIKE. No one's thinking when he's green, Mum.

TESS. I don't know.

MIKE. Anyway. Anyway. Jesus. I'm twenty. It's 1998. It's December 27th. Christmas has been... fine. But to be honest, at this point I am hanging on by a thread, because Christmas Eve is drinks with old schoolfriends, Christmas Day is Christmas Day, with all the usual indulgences, and someone then had the brilliant idea of having a Boxing Day stag do, which is just... There are twelve in the bachelor party, plus the groom, and we make a somewhat misshapen baker's dozen. Three of us share the 'Best Man' mantle: Frazer, Hamish's oldest friend, currently unemployed and an absolute liability, Gordon, a flatmate from medical school, posh and loud, prone to playing devil's advocate and public urination, and then there's me, because Hamish has no male relatives of a similar age and wants someone to fill the family spot. It's a very sweet gesture, but one we both know he didn't really want to make and I didn't really want to accept, but here we are.

ALICE. That isn't true either. He's very fond of you.

MIKE. And that remains entirely not the point. Now anyone who genuinely enjoys a straight man's stag do is a psychopath, that's a given, that is scientific fact. You get the impression that everyone present has dialled up their masculinity by at least twenty per cent because that's what the occasion demands. I am the youngest, the quietest, the queerest, still the outsider despite being on home turf, and it's only about fifteen minutes into our Wetherspoons breakfast that the first shout of 'down it fresher' rings out, and I'm handed a glass of bright-pink unidentifiable alcohol.

Song: 'The Twelve Hours of Stag Do'

ON THE FIRST HOUR OF STAG DO
SOME DICKHEAD BOUGHT FOR ME
AN ICED WATERMELON DAIQUIRI

ON THE SECOND HOUR OF STAG DO
THESE DICKHEADS GOT FOR ME
TOO MUCH GIN
AND AN ICED WATERMELON DAIQUIRI

BY THE THIRD HOUR OF STAG DO
THESE DICKHEADS GOT FOR ME
THREE MULLED WINES
TOO MUCH GIN
AND AN ICED WATERMELON DAIQUIRI

BY THE FOURTH –

TESS. Please don't do all twelve. Come on.

MIKE. This is my story.

TESS. No, it's Mum's story, and you're not telling it right.

MIKE. Fine. Fine. I'll skip ahead. So it starts at Wetherspoons.
It moves on to paintballing in a forest, and it's wet and
freezing and the operators clearly hate us for stealing their
Boxing Day, which is absolutely fair enough. There is a
dreadful turkey curry, and an even worse sprout curry, which
is charmingly advertised as the 'poofter's option'. There are
pubs and clubs and bars that I'm delighted to say I have no
memory of. And somehow it's the end of the night:

BY THE TWELFTH HOUR OF STAG DO
THOSE DICKHEADS BOUGHT FOR ME
TWELVE-YEAR-OLD WHISKY
ELEVEN PER CENT LAGER
TEN TEQUILA SLAMMERS
NINE SLIPPERY NIPPLES
EIGHT VODKA SODAS
SEVEN BLOODY MARYS
SIX PACK OF CARLING
BEER IN A SHOE! (FOR SOME REASON)
FOUR LOCAL ALES
THREE MULLED WINES
TOO MUCH GIN
AND AN ICED WATERMELON DAIQUIRI

We wake groggily and far too early for anyone's liking, but
the multiple alarms finally do their job, and the big day is upon
us. The groom looks pale but in one piece – no broken bones,
second thoughts or overnight tattoos. The plan is for bacon
sarnies and Bloody Marys to set us up for the day, and spirits
are genuinely high – festive – celebratory. It's a Christmas

miracle. And then a text comes through. We've done okay, but the bride… The bride is nowhere to be seen.

Beat.

Good, right? Still no word from them?

TESS. Nothing yet. You're just stopping there, are you?

MIKE. I can pause for dramatic effect too.

TESS. Gran?

ALICE (*through a mouthful of cake*). No, carry on.

MIKE. What have you got there?

ALICE (*hiding this*). Nothing.

MIKE. Clearly not nothing.

ALICE. It's malt loaf – nobody else likes it.

MIKE. Outrageous. Unacceptable. The betrayal.

TESS (*cutting in dramatically*). 'Twas the night before Christmas!

MIKE. Oh, it's like that, is it?

TESS. It's my turn!

MIKE. Sure – go ahead.

TESS. Right. Okay. Ahem.
    'Twas the night before Christmas, and all over town
    Not a creature was stirring, not even…

MIKE. Go on.

TESS. …a sound.

MIKE. Almost.

TESS. And the stockings are hung on the… the old fireplace
    In hope that St Nicholas… might show his face?

MIKE. Wrong, but still impressive.

TESS. My story rhymes – it's harder.

MIKE. Just thought you might know it by now.

TESS. Shut up. I do.
    'Twas the night before… MOUSE! Yes – got it –
    'Twas the night before Christmas, and all through the *house*
    Not a creature was stirring, not even a mouse
    Stocking, stocking, stocking –
    And the children are tucked up all snug in their beds
    With visions of sugar plums – apparently – filling their heads.

MIKE. Better.

TESS. Sugar plums, as we all know, a very popular festive treat back in the day.

ALICE. Do we need the running commentary?

TESS. It's part of the whole… (*Out.*) Okay, look, so here's the thing. 'The Night Before Christmas' isn't the best poem – never liked it as a kid, don't know why – never one of the Christmas books I wanted to read. But then Mum, Mum started changing it, making jokes, doing all the interjections – lots of silly voices. Prancer became Liverpudlian, for some reason, and got a far bigger part than is traditional. And the best thing was she put me in it too. There was little baby Tess in this supposedly dead silent house where not even mice were stirring, knocking things over and making a racket, exasperating Father Christmas to the point of distraction, who just wants to fill the stockings up and be on his way. And it's… it's the way she tells it. And I'd crack up, crease up just at the thought of it. And I can't do her justice – it isn't the same.

MIKE. That's okay.

TESS. But the fun – the fun is in trying to capture that spirit of… Maybe it's stupid.

ALICE. It isn't. Go on.

TESS. But it's about a time when… Cos I'm not that same little girl any more – the house isn't the same – there's crappy high-fibre cereal instead of Coco Pops and gym equipment where my doll's house used to be, and even the sacred Christmas stuff – we don't have coloured fairy lights in the windows any more, because apparently the white ones are classier, and that is just sacrilege, but… I know I don't live here any more, so maybe I don't have a say, but coming home last year to a million tiny little changes, it was the weirdest thing. (*Beat.*) Yes. I've got it.

MIKE. Got what?

TESS. New story. Right:
    'Twas the night before Christmas, two thousand eighteen
    No solitary sighting of snow to be seen
    The mulled wine and mistletoe makes us all loony
    And I've just arrived home from my first term at uni
    Both parents are working, which is no surprise
    But the cupboards are groaning with cheer and mince pies
    So I stuff myself silly with seasonal grub
    My stomach well-lined for a night down the pub.

ALICE. Is this going to be another story that revolves around alcohol?

MIKE. It's Christmas. (*To* TESS.) Go on.

TESS. There's a handful of options, but with any luck
    Nick Green will be serving at the old Dog and Duck
    With his over-moussed hair and his skinny black jeans
    I've fancied this boy since I first turned fourteen.

MIKE. I don't need to hear this.

TESS. I'm letting the muse flow through me.

MIKE. Right.

TESS. And I know it's all fake, and I know he's a flirt
    But I'm still at the bar in a short denim skirt
    There's ice on the ground, but inside there's a fire
    And my face and my loins are aflame with desire.

ALICE. Honestly.

TESS. Now the term has been good, I've got few regrets
    I've been to some classes, I've racked up some debts
    I've made some new friends, I've kissed a few boys
    I've conducted myself with acceptable poise
    And I know that my mum will be surely bereft
    When she sees that I'm not the same child who left
    But these three months away really changed me somehow
    No doubt in my mind I'm a new woman now.
    The pub's full to bursting, but Nick Green has seen me

He gives me a wink and says 'still on Lambrini?'
But I'm not that girl, so I do something risky
I scoff and I smile and I order a whisky.
He smirks as he pours, and Christ, he's a charmer
His dark soulful eyes piercing my armour
And he asks what I'm up to – am I on a date?
I blush and say no, just meeting some mates.
They'll be getting here soon – I'm not quite sure when.
And he asks 'you excited for Christmas then?'

Song: 'A Waiting Song'

AND I DON'T KNOW WHAT TO SAY
I DON'T KNOW WHAT TO DO
I AM RARELY TONGUE-TIED LIKE THIS
CAN'T ARTICULATE
THE FESTIVE TREPIDATION TO A NIGHT LIKE THIS
AND WILL TOO MUCH HAVE CHANGED?
HOME SHOULD BE BORING, HOME IS SAFE

MIKE *takes over.*

MIKE. I DON'T KNOW WHAT TO SAY
I DON'T KNOW WHAT TO DO
MY SISTER IS A NIGHTMARE
AND I CAN'T OVERSTATE
HOW ALL OF THIS IS UTTERLY PREDICTABLE
SO I MUST SAVE THE DAY
I GUESS AT HOME THINGS NEVER CHANGE

ALICE *picks it up.*

ALICE. AND WATCHING AND WAITING
IS HER SECOND NATURE NOW
AND SHE BARELY FEELS THE HOURS SLIPPING BY

SHE IS COSY, SHE IS WARM
IN THE CALM BEFORE THE STORM
AND ON A NIGHT LIKE THIS THE TIME CAN FLY

ALL. AND IT'S CHRISTMAS AFTER ALL
AND MAYBE SNOW WILL FALL
IT CERTAINLY SEEMS COLD ENOUGH TONIGHT

BUT WE NEEDN'T FEAR THE CHILL
FOR THE EVENING HOLDS NO ILL

NO I THINK THIS TIME WE'RE GOING TO BE ALRIGHT
I THINK THIS TIME WE'RE GOING TO BE ALRIGHT

I'M PRETTY SURE THIS TIME WE'LL BE ALRIGHT

A shift. The song ends and ALICE *settles back into her story.*

ALICE. The stars had been blazing bright all evening –

TESS. That's it, Gran – get back in there.

ALICE. Bright in the night sky,
  Ancient and incandescent
  Where the old gods strung them out like lanterns
  There to guide weary travellers home.
  But now she watches through a little round window
  As the fog starts to roll in
  And one by one they're snuffed out.
  No matter. Stars aren't relied upon any more.
  The walls are still thick and the stove still warm
  But there has been talk of a storm to come.
  No matter. No matter.
  The lighthouse lantern turns round and around,
  Casting its watchful eye over the waters
  It won't be long now
  And somewhere,
  Somewhere out there on the endless ocean
  Her husband sails, plotting a course to her.
  Compass and sextant, radar and sonar,
  And her heartbeat out there calling.
  The winds are picking up.
  No matter. No matter. No matter.
  His ship is sturdy, the route familiar
  He could navigate these waters in his sleep
  Don't let him sleep. Don't let him sleep.
  The waters are dark, the waters are deep,
  And one slip, one nod of the head,
  One momentary lapse could bring calamity
  But he is so close now
  He must be so close now
  There's been no word on the wireless
  Only talk of the storm,
  Of the fog, and the winds picking up
  No matter. No matter.

No matter. No matter.
Thunder rumbles above her
Like the crunch of creaking bones
Of the old gods cracking their knuckles
The grumble of ancient throats being cleared
In preparation for…
She dare not think what it might be for
She can only wait and watch the waters
Brief glimpses of the waters as the lantern turns.

TESS. Jesus Christ, Gran, this has got dark.

ALICE. Language.

MIKE. No, she's right. This is hard-core.

ALICE. What's the matter now?

TESS. Seriously, if this is the version of the story you told to
    Mum, she'd have been taken into care.

ALICE. Well forgive me for… for…

TESS. What happened to Christmas? What happened to the fire
    burning? Literally two minutes ago it was all 'cosy and
    warm and the evening holds no ill' and now –

MIKE. Dangerously off-piste, I'd say.

ALICE. Stories change.

TESS. No. No, we're doing this one properly. Where are we?
    She waits by the cosy fire, with the ruby-red wine, and the
    smell of Christmas –

MIKE. That fills every corner –

TESS. Every corner, even though there aren't corners –

MIKE. Because the room is round.

TESS. So – yes – so without any corners to hide in, the smell of
    Christmas hangs all *around* her instead, like a… like a hug in
    a festive jumper.

MIKE. Like a wreath threaded with tinsel.

TESS. Like a moat of custard swimming around a Christmas
    pudding.

MIKE. Warm and sweet and comforting.

TESS. Yes! (*To* ALICE.) You see, Gran – that's how it goes.

ALICE. Fine. Carry on then.

MIKE. Are you okay?

ALICE. Yes, of course.

TESS. It was just a bit intense. For Christmas. Not being critical.

MIKE. We haven't even got to the mouse yet.

TESS. Oh God, the mouse! (*To audience*.) The mouse is the best bit.

MIKE. So she sees this little mouse while she's waiting, and she's scared of it at first –

TESS. But then she catches it –

MIKE. Yes, she catches it, and she's going to release it outside, but it's snowing –

TESS. Yes – ooh, but also, side-point, Gran – it is snowing by this point. It isn't all this fog and thunder and creaky god bones, whatever all that was about – it's magic Christmas snow.

ALICE. Yes, you're right.

MIKE. Right, so – it's snowing, magical Christmas snow, but it's cold – it's still so cold –

TESS. Cold as a choc-ice.

MIKE. Yes! And the little mouse is shivering, curled up into a ball –

TESS. And looks up at her with its tiny little mouse eyes, and says –

MIKE (*in a poor Dutch accent*). Excuse me, kind lady –

TESS. Er, what was that?

MIKE. That's how the mouse talks.

TESS. No, the mouse is Scottish.

MIKE. No.

TESS. Yes! (*An equally poor Scottish accent.*) 'Och aye, I'm a timid wee beastie, who – '

MIKE. No, because it's the little mouse with clogs on from a windmill in old Amsterdam.

TESS. How did it get there from Amsterdam?

MIKE. It's a... On a... a steamer.

TESS. A steamer?

MIKE. It's a well-travelled mouse. Why is it Scottish?

TESS. Robbie Burns.

MIKE. What about him?

TESS. He wrote a... an ode to a... Gran!

MIKE. Mum – tell her.

ALICE (*clears her throat*). And just as she was about to put the little field mouse down, it looked up at her, its black eyes streaming, and its wet nose twitching, and its big ears quivering in the cold. And it said –

ALICE *adopts something akin to a Cornwall/Devon/ Somerset 'farmer' accent.*

'Forgive me, young miss, I don't mean to intrude
I'm sorry to trespass – I hope it's not rude
But it's so cold outside, and so if you please
Could I not help you wait with some biscuits and cheese?'

TESS *and* MIKE *applaud.*

MIKE. Field mouse – makes sense.

TESS. Love it.

MIKE. I forgot that the mouse spoke in rhyme too.

TESS. See – we can both do the rhyming – it's only you who can't.

ALICE (*ignoring this*). And so she takes the little mouse inside
Finds a soft woollen glove and places it near the stove
A warm and cosy nest for her newfound friend
She takes a truckle of cheese from the cupboard –

TESS. Such a good word.

ALICE. Wensleydale and cranberry – and the mouse nods in
     approval.
     The soothing sounds of a choir waft from the radio
     And for a moment, all seems well.

MIKE. Right, okay. Good. Are we back on slightly less
     terrifying ground now?

TESS. Did we save Christmas?

MIKE. I think we just saved Christmas. Mum – you want to
     carry on?

ALICE. No, why don't you carry on with yours?

MIKE. Sure thing. Okay, where was I?

TESS. Morning after – Mum's disappeared.

MIKE. Yes – thank you. So, this is what we know: last solid
     sighting, The Saracen's Head around kicking-out time, where
     they'd run roughshod over Christmas karaoke and been
     necking an experimental eggnog-based cocktail dubbed 'The
     Immaculate Conception'. Spirits high and finding their second
     wind, they decide to head to The Star on the high street,
     because Gail's bridesmaid Gabriella's brother-in-law is the
     owner and she reckons if they sneak in under the wire there
     might be the chance of a cheeky lock-in. This is clearly a
     terrible idea but it seems to have carried momentum, and so
     off they went, Gabriella leading the way, fluffy angel wings
     now bedraggled, halo askew, striding off into the night.

TESS. How much of this story is true, as a rough percentage?

MIKE. One hundred per cent true. My big sister is meant to be
     getting married in just a few hours' time, but both her and her
     hens have flown the coop. Hamish is clearly starting to panic.
     Gordon senses a power vacuum and decides to jump in,
     declaring 'don't worry, big man, we've got this', and striding
     to the door with the kind of blind confidence unique to the
     privately educated. Frazer is having none of this, and before
     I know it, he's on his feet too, blocking Gordon's way. 'Stand
     down, pal. I've had the training.' Gordon asks 'what training?',
     and without missing a beat Frazer stares straight into his soul
     and says 'I can't tell you that. Never ask me that again.' Then

follows a brief stand-off where both men realise neither of them have a clue where to start, and finally Hamish's eyes fall on me. 'Mickey, you're local – you know her – what do you reckon?' I don't have the foggiest, but I know I need to come up with something. 'Last known location,' I offer without conviction, and they follow me to The Star.

TESS. I swear this gets more ridiculous every year.

MIKE. Shush. We're getting to the good bit now.

Song: 'Five Gold Rings'

ON THE FIRST DAY OF CHRISTMAS
MY TRUE LOVE SENT TO ME
A MILE-A-MINUTE FESTIVE
MISSING-PERSON MYSTERY
AND I KNOW NOBODY'S NUPTIALS
ARE EVER ALL STRESS-FREE
BUT I'M SWEATING LIKE A SNOWMAN
WHEN IT'S THIRTY-FIVE DEGREES

(FIVE GOLD RINGS!)
JUST FIVE MINUTES MORE
I SWEAR THAT'S ALL I NEED
(FIVE GOLD RINGS!)
JUST FIVE MINUTES MORE
NOW BRING IT HOME TO ME

We race down to The Star and hammer on the door. Eventually, begrudgingly, someone answers. Not Gabriella's brother-in-law, but the other owner, a formidable matriarch by the name of Denise, who tells us to get lost, don't we read English, and they don't start serving breakfast till eleven. We explain the situation, but it does little to soften her. Transpires she does remember them, and that isn't necessarily a good thing, because they most certainly outstayed their welcome. Now The Star does have a small number of rooms above the pub, and they'd wanted to crash there, but they were too messy and too many at this point, and so… there was no room at the inn.

TESS. Oh God, that's awful.

MIKE. Quiet. And so, in the early hours of the morning they'd been sent packing again. Denise points us in the vague direction she thinks they went, which at first doesn't seem like much help, but then it hits me. I know exactly where she is. I've cracked it – I'm going to find my sister.

ON THE FIRST DAY OF WEDLOCK
IT'S NEVER A GOOD SIGN
WHEN THE BRIDE-TO-BE IS NOWHERE TO BE SEEN
AND THE GROOM RAIDS THE CHURCH
FOR COMMUNION WINE
THERE'S WORK TO DO BUT I PROMISE YOU
IT'S ALL GOING TO BE FINE
GET OUT MY FACE BUT I'M ON THE CASE
AND WE'RE RUNNING OUT OF TIME

(FIVE GOLD RINGS!)
JUST FIVE MINUTES MORE
BEFORE THE BELLS WILL CHIME
(FIVE GOLD RINGS!)
JUST FIVE MINUTES MORE
FOR THE FATES TO REALIGN

Important things to know about Gail, other than the fact that she's a sloppy drunk and an absolute liability – she has a lot of love to give. She has love for all living creatures, and before she started healing humans, she had a borderline obsession with helping animals. This passion blossomed at a small city farm a stone's throw from our parents' house, where she used to volunteer and spend every spare waking moment. If she was ever stressed, or upset, or anxious or just needed to surround herself with a feeling of love and safety and familiarity that is where she'd go – to the farm, to the stables, to the donkeys and the sheep and the cattle a-lowing. And would you believe it, but that farm lies in the very same direction Denise from The Star pointed us.

ON THE FIRST DAY OF CHRISTMAS
I'LL GIVE YOU IF I MAY
MY SWEET HUNGOVER SISTER
WHO'S BEEN SLEEPING IN THE HAY
AND I'M SURE SHE STILL FEELS LIKE THE ASS
UP TO THIS VERY DAY
BUT NO TIME TO TEASE, COME WITH ME PLEASE
BECAUSE WE CAN'T DELAY

(FIVE GOLD RINGS!)
HEAR THE BELLS RING OUT
COS IT'S YOUR WEDDING DAY
(FIVE GOLD RINGS!)
WE'RE THE THREE WISE MEN
AND WE DIDN'T COME TO PLAY

She's curled up amongst the hay bales with her two maids of honour, a small donkey gently nuzzling at her toes –

(FIVE GOLD RINGS!)
HEAR THE ANGELS SING
AND MAKE THE YULETIDE GAY
(FIVE GOLD RINGS!)
CALL ME SANTA
COS YOU KNOW I'VE COME TO SLAY

TESS. Gran, is any of this even a little bit true?

ALICE. They stayed with her friend Bethan who lived next door to the sanctuary.

MIKE. No, she slept with the oxen and I saved the wedding.

ALICE (to TESS). She lost her phone and your father panicked.

MIKE. That isn't what happened.

ALICE. If I recall it was a lot of fuss over nothing.

MIKE. Um, did I try to ruin your story?

ALICE. Yes. Constantly.

MIKE. Anyway. Anyway, the point is I found her, and we all didn't we – we all lived happily ever after.

ALICE. I suppose.

MIKE. So, round of applause for me, in essence.

TESS. What happened to Dean?

MIKE. Hmm?

TESS. Dean whatsit – the Liam Gallagher boy?

MIKE. Oh. Oh God, he… He flirted with me for six months, dated a long string of awful women and dropped out the following summer.

TESS. Fair enough.

MIKE. Moving on. Dog and Duck?

TESS. Oh, right, sure. Let's see...
So I'm nursing my Scotch, still trying to sip it
He raises an eyebrow, I tell him to zip it
We've got this connection, it's top-level bants
And it helps that I want to get into his pants
But it's more than just that – it's safe and he's sound
And I'm starting to feel on familiar ground.
He asks how I've been, he asks after Mum,
He's happy to see me, he pours me a rum,
We're definitely sparking, but then right on cue
A bang at the door and a hullabaloo –
There's Gemma and Ollie and Donna and Stacey
There's Wilson and Whitey and Tina and Tracey
The whole gang pile in for a night on the town
Where we sack off our families and let our hair down
And wily old Nick, still immune to my passes
Slinks off to the kitchen to go clean some glasses.
They're a sight for sore eyes – I've been missing them lots
We squeal and we hug and we line up the shots
And I am a bit quiet for a minute, for sure
But it doesn't take long for the weirdness to thaw
Soon we start swapping stories, we're having a ball,
And it's quickly like I never left here at all.
Gemma is wasted, and single again,
And Donna is currently dating three men
And Stacey and Tracey, two birds of a feather,
Are currently plotting a business together
(Specifics are hazy, they've still got to plan it
But it's something with dogs and it's definitely organic.)
There's so much to tell me, and so much has changed
But it's comforting seeing so much is the same.
And then it's my turn – so what am I scheming?
Known in the group as I am for daydreaming
And I have got some news, but before I get going
Whitey looks up and says 'Jesus, it's snowing'
It's only a dusting, but it gets a cheer
And the group are decided we're all staying here
We won't risk the blizzard – we're going to ground

And Gemma is up to get in the next round.
I glance at my phone, and I see Mum has texted
And given her shift that is quite unexpected
But it seems there's a mix-up, she isn't sure how
But the night has been covered – she's finishing now
And in fifteen minutes she's going to be home –
Would be nice to see me, if I'm on my own.
I say I've got plans – I'm out with my friends
And tricky to tell when this kind of night ends
We'll chat in the morning, or later, we'll see
But either way, she shouldn't wait up for me.
She says not to worry – she tells me 'have fun',
And there's plenty to eat in the house when I'm done.
She's got in those biscuits that only I like,
Then adds 'Merry Christmas' and 'have a good night'.

Can I just say, rhyming gets exhausting after a bit.

MIKE. You okay?

TESS. Yeah, just taking a breather.

TESS *glances at her phone*.

ALICE. Any news?

TESS. Still waiting.

MIKE. You know she wouldn't have minded you staying out –
    your mum – she'd never –

TESS. I know.

MIKE. You were here a lot, weren't you – over the holidays?

TESS. Yeah.

MIKE. Was a good one last year. That custard.

TESS. Oh my God.

ALICE. Don't remind me.

TESS (*out*). Last year Gran quote-unquote 'accidentally' made
    a jug of custard entirely with Baileys instead of cream, and it
    was I swear to God the best thing I've ever tasted.

MIKE. Baileys is mostly cream anyway.

TESS. True. (*Beat.*) Did anyone else want to…? Gran?

ALICE. Hmm?

TESS. Lighthouse Keeper?

ALICE. I don't think so.

TESS. Go on.

ALICE. I think this has maybe all got a little... I think we've all outgrown these stories somewhat, haven't we?

MIKE. Course we haven't.

ALICE. Considering I've been told I'm telling mine all wrong, yours is entirely fabricated, and hers bears no resemblance to 'The Night Before Christmas' whatsoever.

TESS. That's just... It isn't...

MIKE. It's okay.

ALICE. I'm not really sure why any of us are –

TESS. I can... No, I can tell – we could read the proper one, we've got, haven't we – there's a box of Christmas books around somewhere, I know there is.

ALICE. No need.

TESS. I didn't mean to spoil anything.

MIKE. You haven't.

TESS. I'm sorry.

MIKE. It's fine. They'll be here soon.

ALICE. Yes.

MIKE (*going to a cupboard*). Here – have some more crisps.

TESS. What've you got?

MIKE (*examining a packet*). Cranberry and frankincense.

TESS. Jesus.

ALICE. I could put some smoked salmon out, if you wanted.

TESS. Now you're talking.

ALICE. I suppose it doesn't matter if –

MIKE. No – you know what, we should wait. They won't be long. We'll wait.

ALICE. If you're sure.

Pause.

MIKE. Y'know I think he went into the police, actually – Dean Whitehead. Added me on Facebook a while back.

TESS. Right.

MIKE. Doesn't dress like Liam Gallagher any more.

TESS. Shame.

MIKE. Not really.

ALICE. I'm sorry if I... I didn't mean to...

ALICE *trails off.*

TESS. So they ring out last orders, it's time we should go
As each of my mates totters off in the snow
We hug our goodbyes and the bar empties quick
And without even planning it's just me and Nick
He gives me a wink, and I know that's the code
With a flash of his smile, he says 'one for the road?'
And I know that I shouldn't, but he's started to pour
So I give him a nod and I mutter a 'sure'.
I'm back on whisky, he's grabbed a beer
And he asks me if it's been a good year.
And this is embarrassing, I can't tell him why
But suddenly I've got a tear in my eye
It must be the hour, it must be the booze,
It must be the snow and some pre-Christmas blues
It must the carols that still softly play
And he takes my hand gently and says 'that's okay'
He says that he's glad that I came in tonight
He says for a while he's been hoping I might
But he had a fear in the back of his mind
That I'd jump at the chance to leave this place behind.
He remembers those nights in this very bar
When I'd always chat shit about travelling far
A drink in my hand, I'd start getting romantic
About setting sail across the Atlantic
Or crossing the Andes, or hiking K2

Or spending a year building schools in Peru
And he's not being mean, and why should I care,
But I blurt out the news I've been dying to share
It's funny he'd say that, because, if you please
I'm actually going to study overseas
I found this exchange scheme – so Christmas next year
I won't even be on the same hemisphere

**Song: 'The Other Side of the World (I Can't Get Used
To That)'**

THIS TIME NEXT YEAR
I'LL BE IN AUSTRALIA
SHH – I'VE NOT TOLD ANYONE YET
NO SWEAT – THEY'D FRET – WOULDN'T GET IT
BUT I'LL GET AWAY
GONNA GET AWAY

TO AUSTRALIA
DRINKING BEER, THROWING SHRIMP ON A BARBIE
IN BRISBANE OR MELBOURNE OR SYDNEY
AND WE CAN SKYPE ON CHRISTMAS DAY
I KNOW EXACTLY WHAT THEY'LL SAY
THEY'LL SAY

IS IT HOT, IS IT LATE, IS IT EARLY?
ARE YOU AHEAD OR ARE YOU BEHIND?
IT BLOWS MY MIND THAT WE CAN DO THIS
FROM THE OTHER SIDE OF THE WORLD

ARE YOU WELL, DID YOU SLEEP, HAVE YOU EATEN?
DID YOU GET THE THINGS I SENT?
I MEANT TO ASK DO THEY DO ADVENT THERE
ON THE OTHER SIDE OF THE WORLD
THE OTHER SIDE OF THE WORLD

I CAN'T GET USED TO THAT
I CAN'T GET USED TO THAT
I CAN'T, I CAN'T

I CAN'T GET USED TO THAT
I CAN'T GET USED TO THAT
I CAN'T, I CAN'T

BUT I'LL BE IN AUSTRALIA
DRINKING FOSTER'S OUT OF A DIDGERIDOO

TENDING BAR
AND GETTING REGRETTABLE TATTOOS
OF KANGAROOS
WHICH SEEMS LIKE THE KIND OF THING
THAT YOU DO

IN AUSTRALIA
GONNA FIND ME A RUGGED OUTBACK-MAN
WITH THE CHARM AND PIZZAZZ OF HUGH JACKMAN
AND WE'D STILL SKYPE ON CHRISTMAS DAY
I KNOW EXACTLY WHAT THEY'D SAY
THEY'LL SAY

MIGHT YOU MAKE IT HOME NEXT YEAR?
I KNOW THAT IT'S A WAY TO GO
BUT ALL OF US WOULD LOVE TO HAVE YOU HERE
WE'D LOVE TO HAVE YOU NEAR

THE NEWSPAPERS ARE SAYING WE'LL GET SNOW
YOU'LL BE ON A BEACH SOMEWHERE
AND WE'LL BE HERE WRAPPED UP LIKE ESKIMOS
THAT'S FUNNY I SUPPOSE
FROM THE SUNNY SIDE OF THE WORLD

BUT I CAN'T GET USED TO THAT
I CAN'T GET USED TO THAT
I CAN'T, I CAN'T

I CAN'T GET USED TO THAT
I CAN'T GET USED TO THAT
I CAN'T, I CAN'T

CAN'T GO TO AUSTRALIA
NO I KNOW THAT IT'S ONLY A STORY
AND I KNOW THEY JUST WANT THE BEST FOR ME
SO I'LL DO JUST AS I'M TOLD
STAY AT HOME AND WATCH THEM BOTH GROW OLD

BUT I CAN'T GET USED TO THAT
I CAN'T GET USED TO THAT
I CAN'T, I CAN'T

I CAN'T, I CAN'T, I CAN'T, I CAN'T

Song ends.

MIKE. I didn't know about that.

TESS. Yeah, well.

MIKE. Did you apply?

TESS. Um, yeah.

MIKE. But – ?

TESS. Yeah. Got accepted, provisionally, but... Never got as far as putting down a deposit or anything.

MIKE. Did you talk to your mum about it?

TESS. It's alright.

MIKE. Because she would've wanted –

TESS. It's fine.

MIKE. You should've at least talked to her.

TESS. I've got a lifetime to go bum around on a beach somewhere, haven't I? It's not a big deal.

MIKE. I presume there was some studying involved too?

TESS. Yeah. I mean it was a proper... They've got really good labs, like this amazing state-of-the-art research centre out there. Looks incredible. (*Beat.*) But I dunno. Warwick's great too. Not quite as hot, but... who wants sunshine at Christmas anyway? It's not right.

MIKE. There'll be other chances, if you want it.

TESS. Yeah.

Beat.

ALICE. I'm sorry, what happened between you and this barman?

TESS. What? Oh, nothing. No, perfect gentleman – put me in a cab and I came home. Mum had fallen asleep in her chair but she woke up while I was taking my shoes off. We had a hot chocolate. It was nice.

MIKE. That bit didn't rhyme.

TESS. Told you – rhyming's hard.

Beat.

ALICE. It's late.
        The stove still glows with the memory of heat
        The candles burnt down low
        The little mouse dozing in his little nest
        But the lighthouse keeper doesn't sleep
        It won't be long now, not long
        And the wind howls, and the room shakes,
        And the snow has turned to hail.
        No matter
        When out of nowhere lightning strikes –
        A bolt from the blue
        A direct strike on the lighthouse roof
        The stone is strong – no harm shall come to her –
        But the lantern –
        The lantern goes out –

On this, TESS *flicks the lights off, sending the room into
darkness.*

MIKE. Tess!

TESS. What? I'm adding drama.

MIKE. Jesus.

ALICE. Language.

TESS. It's what Mum used to do.

ALICE. And the lighthouse keeper knows this is disaster,
        Because somewhere out there on the endless ocean
        Her lover sails, heading home to her
        Any moment now he could arrive.
        The waters here are treacherous,
        Swirling currents and hidden rocks,
        The lighthouse the only guide to safe passage
        Without her light, he has no hope of survival.
        What can she do?
        She must do *something* – there must be a solution
        She must find a way to make this right
        Because the alternative is unthinkable.
        And out there on the endless ocean
        Her lover knows he's close
        The wind has ceased to chill him
        The thunder holds no fear

Because he is almost home
And he can picture the glow of the fire,
Smell the orange and clove,
Taste the Christmas pudding –
He is looking for the light that he knows must be there
The light that could never go out
He hasn't spotted it yet
No matter, no matter,
He knows the way
So on into the darkness he sails
As the storm swells
And the waters froth and foam beneath him.
Onwards, onwards, ever onwards
Pushing all thought of fear from his mind.

Song: 'I Will Wait for You'

AND HE TURNED FROM THE SPRAY
AND THE WIND AND THE WAVE
AND THE THUNDER THAT FORKED
THROUGH THE SKY

AND HE CRIED OUT IN PAIN
AS THE BITTEREST RAIN
STUNG HIS EYES

AND THE OCEAN IT ROARED
LIKE IT NE'ER HAD BEFORE
AS THE WATERS GREW HIGHER AND HIGHER

BUT THEN OVER THE STORM
CAME A VOICE BRIGHT AND WARM
AS A FIRE

AND THE VOICE WAS SINGING

I WILL WAIT FOR YOU ALWAYS
I WILL WAIT FOR YOU ALWAYS, ALWAYS

I WILL WAIT FOR YOU ALWAYS
I WILL WAIT FOR YOU ALWAYS, ALWAYS

For there, somewhere in the distance
In the deep, dark distance
The lighthouse keeper is singing,
Singing to shout down the storm.

She climbs out onto the roof
Through a small round hatch
And the wind howls
And the stone creaks
And the metal is scorched from where the lightning struck.
Everything is frozen, slippery,
One false move and she could plummet
And wet and unwieldy she holds under one arm
The replacement lantern
If only she can make it in time.

FOR THERE IN THE GALE
WITH THE SLEET AND THE HAIL
SHE COULD SEE A FEW METRES AT MOST

BUT OH, FOR THIS MAN
SHE WOULD NEVER ABANDON HER POST

THE FOG WAS SO THICK
AND THE CURRENT SO QUICK
AND THE NIGHT SO IMPOSSIBLY DARK

BUT THERE ON THE ROOF
SHE SANG OUT THE TRUTH
IN HER HEART

AND THE SONG SHE'S SINGING:

I WILL WAIT FOR YOU ALWAYS
I WILL WAIT FOR YOU ALWAYS, ALWAYS

I WILL WAIT FOR YOU ALWAYS
I WILL WAIT FOR YOU ALWAYS, ALWAYS

TESS. And I don't know why, because it isn't this, but in my
mind I always picture King Kong clinging onto the Empire
State Building.

MIKE. Luke Skywalker at the end of *The Empire Strikes Back*.

TESS. Something sort of desperate and sad about it.

ALICE. And a foot slips
    She lurches, lunges,
    Fingers numb with cold but just manage to find purchase
    But the lantern – the last lantern – is lost

Crashing down to the rocks below
Her last hope, smashed to smithereens beneath her
Matches sodden, no flint, no fuel, no way to make a flame
And she feels a light within her start to fizzle out
As she pictures a ship somewhere out there in the darkness
Almost on top of her now
No way of knowing what they're sailing into.
And in that moment –

TESS. And this is definitely the bit in *The Matrix* where he puts his hand out to stop the bullets. It's the bit when you realise the power was in you all along, because –

ALICE. She opens her mouth
And more than words, more than a wail
More than a song –
Light comes pouring out of her,
A blazing beam of impossible light that pierces the darkness
That is meant for one soul, and one soul only
And he sees it, because how could he not see it?
Her light, her love, blazing and brilliant,
Never in question, never in doubt,
A light that would always find him, and guide him home.

ALL. I WILL WAIT FOR YOU ALWAYS
I WILL WAIT FOR YOU ALWAYS, ALWAYS

I WILL WAIT FOR YOU ALWAYS
I WILL WAIT FOR YOU ALWAYS, ALWAYS

MIKE *and* TESS *continue harmonies under next section of narration.*

ALICE. And the waters calm
And the wind dies down
And the rain changes to gentle flakes of snow
And he is mooring the boat now
Up against the little lighthouse that smells of Christmas
And she stands on the threshold to greet him.

Song ends. A beat. TESS*'s phone buzzes.*

TESS. They're in the car.

ALICE. Oh, thank God.

TESS. They're setting off now.

MIKE. Was there a – ?

TESS. Just the normal stuff. Just forms and waiting to talk to –

MIKE. Right.

TESS. But it's all good.

ALICE. I'll get some things warming up.

MIKE. Traffic will be a nightmare.

ALICE. They shouldn't rush.

TESS. He won't.

ALICE. Tell him to drive safe – to take it slowly.

TESS. He will.

MIKE. Did I see cheese straws earlier?

ALICE. Yes. Top cupboard. Put some in a bowl.

MIKE. On it.

ALICE. And, um, some nuts – the smoked nuts she likes.

TESS. She probably won't be that hungry.

ALICE. In the silver packet – her favourites.

TESS. Her appetite isn't... Don't be offended if –

ALICE. I won't.

MIKE (*to* TESS). And your dad will hoover up anything going.

TESS. True.

ALICE. We haven't even laid the table. All this time, and we still haven't –

TESS. It's fine.

ALICE. There are crackers, and napkins, and –

MIKE. We've still got a while, even if the traffic's good.

ALICE. Yes.

TESS. I think... I think we should tell them.

MIKE. What?

TESS. Explain what's really going on.

ALICE. What do you mean?

TESS. You know what I mean.

ALICE. They won't be long now.

MIKE. I don't think we have to, do we?

TESS. I think we should. (*Out.*) When your mum's a doctor and your dad's a paramedic you grow up seeing life a bit differently. Sometimes they would walk death into the house with them – never meant to, but you can't always help it. You take a breath and stamp your feet and try to wipe all traces of it off on the doormat, but sometimes it still slips in. And that's… okay. That's fine, actually.

ALICE. I had my reservations, I did, when she told us she wanted to study medicine. She was bright enough, of course, and kind, and meticulous, all of that, but… and especially the emergency room. I couldn't. I wouldn't last a day. And I did have my doubts whether… but I was wrong, of course.

MIKE. And Hamish is… I don't think you can overestimate how important it is, actually, to have someone else who gets it, who knows where you're coming from, who's seen it all too. And he's brilliant. I'd never say it in front of either of them, but he's been brilliant.

TESS. When your mum is a doctor and your dad's a paramedic you do some things differently – like Christmas. You grab the hours when you can. You get used to waiting, and missing things, and not always being the number-one priority. You hear a lot of 'oh, could your mother not make it?' 'Where's your mum today?' 'She's at the hospital. Yeah, she's back at the hospital again.' Mum's been at the hospital a lot lately. Mum's been…

MIKE. You don't have to.

ALICE. My daughter has been unwell.

MIKE. You don't have to say what. That's not important.

ALICE. No.

TESS. And hospitals, they try really hard to empty out as many patients as they can before Christmas. No one wants to be there, of course they don't, so if they can't find a way to discharge that means it's serious. That means it's really bad. And we didn't know, we weren't sure whether...

MIKE. But she's on her way.

TESS. She is, yeah.

MIKE. It was looking touch-and-go for a bit, but –

ALICE. But anyway, the point is it's all sorted now.

TESS. And when she gets here we'll go through all of this all over again. The same old stories, all over again.

ALICE. She's going to have questions about this barman.

TESS. I'm going to ask her where the mouse is really from.

ALICE. What does she know about that?

MIKE. All of this all over again. And the next time, and the time after, as many times as there are. As many times as we have.

ALICE. And there'll be no complaining –

TESS. Well that's not true.

ALICE. There'll be minimal complaints.

MIKE. Um –

ALICE. We'll all be happy to hear them, even though we've heard them before. Because we've heard them before. Because that's why they're told. Because that's us. No more waiting. They'll be home very soon.

Song: 'The Last Time'

ALL. IF THIS IS THE LAST TIME
I'M WITH YOU
IF THIS IS THE LAST TIME
WE ALL COME TOGETHER LIKE THIS
WILL YOU PROMISE ME
IT WON'T BE ANY DIFFERENT?
WE'LL TELL THE SAME OLD STORIES

AND PRETEND WE HAVEN'T NOTICED
IT'S GOT DARK OUTSIDE
THE DAYS ARE SHORTER NOW

TESS. AND THERE'S NOTHING YOU CAN DO
ABOUT THAT

ALICE. THERE'S NOTHING YOU CAN SAY
TO CHANGE THE THINGS WE WISH WEREN'T TRUE

MIKE. BUT NONE OF THAT MATTERS
WHEN I'M WITH YOU

ALL. IF THIS IS THE LAST TIME
I'M WITH YOU
IF THIS IS THE LAST TIME
WE ALL COME TOGETHER LIKE THIS
MIKE. I STILL PROMISE
I WON'T LET YOU WIN AT RUMMIKUB
YOU'LL GET NO SPECIAL TREATMENT
TESS. WE'LL JUST HUG A LITTLE LONGER
WHEN IT'S TIME TO LEAVE
YOU WON'T WANT ANY FUSS

ALICE. COS THERE'S NOTHING YOU CAN DO ABOUT IT

ALICE/TESS. THERE'S NOTHING YOU CAN SAY
TO CHANGE THE THINGS WE WISH WEREN'T TRUE

ALL. BUT NONE OF THAT MATTERS WHEN I'M
WITH YOU
NONE OF THAT MATTERS WHEN I'M WITH YOU

TESS. RING OUT THOSE BELLS
ALICE/MIKE.   WE DON'T MIND WAITING
ALICE.   TELL ME ONE MORE STORY
TESS/MIKE. SING OF CHRISTMAS TIME
TESS. AND ALL THE THINGS WE ALWAYS DO
MIKE.   I PROMISE I WON'T INTERRUPT
MIKE/ALICE.   FROM ALL THE YEARS PAST
TESS. WE'LL DO IT ALL AGAIN

ALL. RING OUT THOSE BELLS
SING OF CHRISTMAS TIME
AND ALL THE CRUCIAL RITUALS
THAT MATTER JUST BECAUSE

RING OUT THOSE BELLS
SING OF CHRISTMAS TIME
AND ALL THE STUPID THINGS WE DO
THAT MEAN THE WORLD TO US

THAT'S CHRISTMAS

End.

MUSIC

Words and Music by Chris Bush
Arrangements by Matt Winkworth

Voice

'It's Christmas'

Words and music by Chris Bush
arr. Matt Winkworth

4   Voice

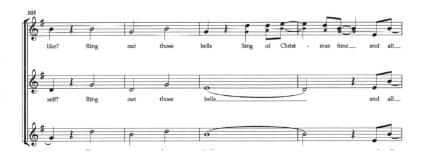

54

Voice

the stu - pid lit - tle things_ that mean the world_ to us_____

That's Christ - mas_____

Voice

'The Twelve Hours of Stag Do'

Music trad. words by Chris Bush
arr. Matt Winkworth

2

Ten te - qui - la slam - mers, Nine slip - p'ry nip - ples,

Eight vod - ka so - das, Se - ven bloo - dy Ma - rys,

Six - pack of Car - ling, Beer in a shoe (for some rea - son)

Four_____ lo - cal ales, Three mulled wines,

Too_____ much_____ gin, And an iced wat - er - mel - on dai - qui -

ri!

4
47–50

16
51–66

Voice

'A Waiting Song'

Words and music by Chris Bush
arr. Matt Winkworth

2

Voice

3   Voice

I think this time we're gon-na be___ al - right   I'm

I think this time we're gon-na be___ al - right   I'm

think this time we're gon-na be___ al - right   I'm

All three: rit. . . . . tempo

pret - ty   sure___   this   time___   we'll   be   al - right

60

'Five Gold Rings'

2

bride-to-be is no where to be seen And the groom raids the church for com-mun-i-on wine There's

work to do___ but I prom-ise you___ It's all gon' to be fine___ Get

out my face but I'm on the case___ and we're run-ning out of time___

3

Five gold___ rings! Just five min-utes more be-fore the bells will chime oh___

A+T:

3

Five gold___ rings!

Five gold___ rings!___ Just five min-utes more for the fates to re-al-ign___

Five gold___ rings!___

On the first day of Christ-mas I'll give you if I may My sweet hung-o-ver sis-ter Who's been

3

sleep - ing   in   the   hay___   And I'm sure she still feels like the ass___ Up

to this ve - ry day   But no time to tease, come with me please Be - cause we can't de - lay_   oh_

Five   gold_____   rings!   Hear the bells ring out_ cos it's your wed-ding day   Oh_

Five   gold_____   rings!

five   gold_____ rings___   We're the three wise men and we did-n't come to play_

Five   gold_____   rings!___

Five   gold_____   rings!   Hear the an-gels sing and make the yule-tide gay   Oh_

Five   gold_____   rings!

V.S.

63

4

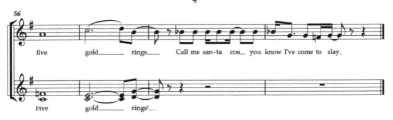

five gold rings Call me san-ta cos_ you know I've come to slay_

Five gold rings!_

Voice

'The Other Side of the World (I Can't Get Used To That)'

Music and words by Chris Bush
arr. Matt Winkworth

Tess:
This time next year I'll be in Au - stra - lia___ Shh I've

not told an - y - one yet No sweat, they'd fret, would-n't get it But I'll get a - way I'm gon-na

get a - way___ To Aus - tra - lia Drink-ing beer, throw-ing shrimp on a bar - bie___ In

Bris-bane or Mel-bourne or Syd - ney___ And we can Skype on Christ-mas Day

___ I know ex - act - ly what they'll say___ 'n' they'll say___ Is it hot, is it

late, is it ear - ly? Are you a - head___ or are you be - hind It blows my mind

___ that we___ can do___ this From the oth-er side___ of the world Are you well, did you

sleep, have you eat - en? And did you get the things I sent?___ I meant to ask

___ do they___ have ad - vent there On the oth -er side___ of the world___ The

V.S.

3

Voice

I know that it's__ a way__ to go But all of us__ would love
__ to have__ you here__ We'd love to have__ you near__
The news - pa - pers are say - ing we'll__ get snow
You'll be on__ a beach__ some-where And we'll be here__ wrapped up__
__ like Es - ki - mos__ That's fun - ny I__ sup pose__ From the
sun - ny side__ of the world But I can't get used to that__ I can't get
used to that__ I__ can't I can't__
Can't go__ to Aus - tra - lia No I know that it's on - ly a sto - ry__ And I
know they just want the best for me__ So I'll do just as I'm told
__ Stay at home and watch them both grow old But__ I can't get

V.S.

4   Voice

used to that___   I can't get used to that___ I___ can't

I can't___   I can't___

I can't___   I can't___

I can't___

2
132–133

Voice

'I Will Wait for You'

Music & Lyrics by Chris Bush
arr. Matt Winkworth

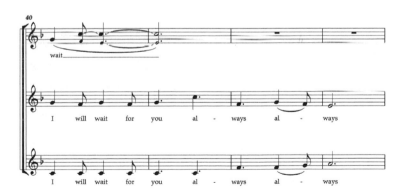

70

Voice

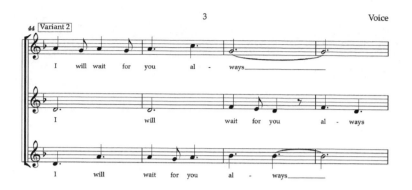

4

Voice

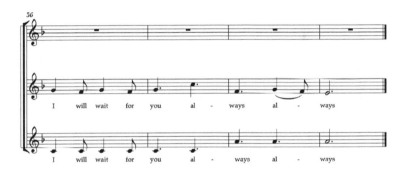

Voice

'The Last Time'